IMAGES
of America

SOUTHERN ARIZONA
MILITARY OUTPOSTS

ON THE COVER: This picture was taken at Bowie, Arizona, when Geronimo was shipped to Florida in September 1886. Lt. Leonard Wood lounges in the foreground (first row, farthest left), and the man in the campaign hat with tall crown (sitting in the second row, second from left) is Capt. Henry W. Lawton, who commanded the 4th U.S. Cavalry, Troop B. This unit served as the escort for Geronimo after his forced relocation to Florida. (National Archives.)

IMAGES
of America

SOUTHERN ARIZONA
MILITARY OUTPOSTS

John P. Langellier

ARCADIA
PUBLISHING

Published by Arcadia Publishing
Charleston, South Carolina

Printed in the United States of America

Library of Congress Control Number: 2010940836

For all general information, please contact Arcadia Publishing:
Telephone 843-853-2070
Fax 843-853-0044
E-mail sales@arcadiapublishing.com
For customer service and orders:
Toll-Free 1-888-313-2665

Visit us on the Internet at www.arcadiapublishing.com

*Dedicated to the memory of my sister Donnita Marie
Bertagnolli (1943–2010), who trekked with our family to
make Arizona our home more than a half-century ago*

CONTENTS

ACKNOWLEDGMENTS

This book was possible because of the assistance of many institutions, including the Kansas State Historical Society, Frontier Army Museum, Library of Congress, National Archives Still Photographs Division, National Park Service, U.S. Army Center of Military History, U.S. Army Military History Institute, and U.S. Cavalry Museum. In Los Angeles, Marva Felchin and Marilyn Kim of the Museum of the American West, Autry National Center, made images from a rare album in the collections there available. At Fort Bowie, Karen Gonzales provided images of the site as it is today. Additionally, Tina Clark and Ann Walker made images available from Yuma Depot. Closer to home, Scott Anderson and Libby Coyner of Sharlot Hall Museum and Kate Reeve at the Arizona Historical Society's library in Tucson all provided many key images. Likewise, Stephen Gregory of the Fort Huachuca Museum went far beyond the call of duty to provide assistance. So, too, did my colleague Fred Veil in making some of his family's heirlooms available, while my cousin George M. Langellier Jr. offered many unpublished pictures from his collection. Rae Whitley graciously took time to provide pictures of the Fort Lowell Museum and the Museum of the Horse Soldier. Mick Woodcock generously read the draft of this volume. Moreover, Jared S. Jackson with Arcadia Publishing was helpful through the entire process. Finally, I am extremely grateful to Dr. Neil Thomas for his extensive technical support that made this publication possible.

INTRODUCTION

In 1846, very soon after war erupted between the United States and Mexico, preparations began for the invasion of Mexican territory at various points. One expedition was to advance from the Missouri River west to Mexico, Santa Fé being the main objective. An additional goal was added: the occupation of Upper California. Brig. Gen. Stephan Watts Kearny was placed in command of this Army of the West, which consisted of Companies B, C, G, I and K, of the 1st U.S. Dragoons, two companies of artillery, two of infantry, and nine companies of Missouri volunteer cavalry under the command of Col. A. W. Doniphan, in all about 1800 men. This command was concentrated at Bent's Fort on the Arkansas River. From there it marched for Santa Fé on August 1, 1846.

The Mexican governor of New Mexico made a token show of resistance, but both Las Vegas and Santa Fé were occupied in mid-August without bloodshed. The Mexicans retreated upon Kearny's approach, and he left Colonel Doniphan in command as he resumed the march for California on September 26.

Kearny's column, which was mounted on mules acquired in New Mexico, advanced westward intent on reaching California by the most direct route. He and 100 soldiers guided by Kit Carson followed the Gila River across today's Arizona on a well-known trail used by earlier trappers and traders. The force faced several almost impassable canyons yet forged forward to the West Coast.

Because of the route's tortuous terrain, Kearny placed his supply wagons under the command of Lt. Col. Philip St. George Cooke and his Mormon Battalion of some 500 foot soldiers recruited from the Church of Latter Day Saints at Council Bluff, Iowa. Following six weeks behind Kearny, Cooke and his men entered Arizona through Guadalupe Pass in the extreme southwestern corner of New Mexico. Thereafter they snaked along the San Pedro River and then came to the small Mexican presidio of Tucson where the local garrison withdrew without a fight to nearby Mission San Xavier del Bac. From there, Cooke paralleled the Santa Cruz River to the Pima villages on the Gila River and proceeded down the Gila floodplain to Yuma Crossing at the Colorado River.

The Mormon Battalion and Kearny's contingent had the distinction of being the largest groups to cross Arizona up to that time. The trails they blazed would be followed by thousands of others, but for some years, the land traversed was seen as an obstacle to reaching the Pacific.

In fact, the military forces that followed focused on finding the best means to reach the neighboring Golden State. Consequently, in 1848, after the Treaty of Guadalupe Hidalgo brought an end to the war, the U.S. government launched a series of expeditions led by army officers to explore, map, and record information about the geography, geology, and natural history of the Southwest. These forays included efforts to secure a railroad route that would help link the nation's southern lands. So it was that, for much of the period following the treaty with Mexico, most of the army's presence was transitory. That situation was about to change.

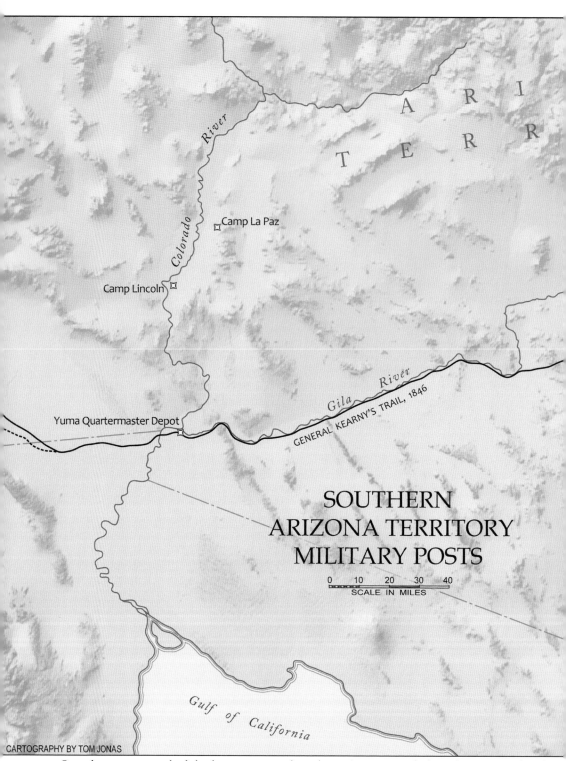

SOUTHERN
ARIZONA TERRITORY
MILITARY POSTS

0   10   20   30   40
SCALE IN MILES

Camp La Paz

Camp Lincoln

Colorado River

Gila River

GENERAL KEARNY'S TRAIL, 1846

Yuma Quartermaster Depot

Gulf of California

A R I
T E R R

CARTOGRAPHY BY TOM JONAS

Seen here are several of the key outposts of southern Arizona, including the routes taken by

Kearny and Cooke during the war with Mexico. (Tom Jonas.)

More than three decades after his initiation as combat commander during the War of 1812, Stephen Watts Kearny led the Army of the Potomac. He and his men trudged from Fort Leavenworth, Kansas, to California via southern Arizona. (National Archives.)

One

MILITARY GARRISONS

The U.S. Army merely passed through southern Arizona in the early years, but in due course, garrisons were established, including Camp Yuma west of the Colorado River in California in 1850. This outpost would be followed by scores of other forts, cantonments, and camps. The often isolated bastions provided military protection, as well as contributed to the local economy and the social life in the areas that surrounded them. Unlike the Hollywood stereotype, they were not wooden stockades. Instead they appeared as small towns with residences, hospitals, stores, and support structures forming a quadrangle around a central parade ground that was akin to a village green. Most of these posts have long since disappeared, but some of the garrisons, such as Fort Huachuca, continue to play a significant role in Arizona to this day.

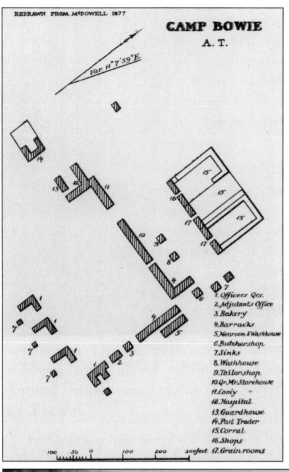

REDRAWN FROM McDOWELL 1877

CAMP BOWIE
A. T.

Var. 11° 7′59″ E.

1. Officers Qrs.
2. Adjutants Office
3. Bakery
4. Barracks
5. Messroom & Washhouse
6. Butchershop
7. Sinks
8. Washhouse
9. Tailorshop
10. Qr.Mr.Storehouse
11. Comy "
12. Hospital
13. Guardhouse
14. Post Trader
15. Corral
16. Shops
17. Grain rooms

100 50 0   100   200   300 feet

Beginning in the 1860s, Fort Bowie guarded nearby Apache Pass. It gradually evolved into a substantial frontier army post, as indicated by this plan from the 1870s that shows a substantial complex of adobe structures. (George M. Langellier Jr.)

Geronimo was held briefly at Fort Bowie as a prisoner of war in 1886 before being transported to Florida. His arrival attracted considerable attention as troopers gather around their former Apache foe near the guardhouse where he was incarcerated. (National Archives.)

85745

This is the 4th U.S. Cavalry band at Fort Bowie on September 8, 1886. When Geronimo and his followers boarded the train to Florida, the band played "Auld Lang Syne." (National Archives.)

A cavalry patrol sets out from Fort Bowie in the early 1890s. They leave the post trader's store behind as they ride off for a routine patrol. (National Archives.)

In 1891, cavalry troopers wearing their impractical white stable outfits march in formation to groom their mounts during stable call at Fort Bowie. (Museum of the American West, Autry National Center, Los Angeles; 93.236.1.)

The 4th U.S. Cavalry band has put aside their brass and drums to form an orchestra capable of playing popular civilian tunes and classical selections. (National Archives.)

During its final years, Fort Bowie's officers and their family members could enjoy many pastimes, such as playing tennis. (Museum of the American West, Autry National Center, Los Angeles; 93.236.1.)

Horseback riding was another means of passing the time for those fortunate enough to enjoy excursions around the surrounding acreage of Fort Bowie. (Museum of the American West, Autry National Center, Los Angeles; 93.236.1.)

Hunting provided one more diversion at Fort Bowie and supplemented the daily diet, although javelina (also known as peccary) was a less popular meat source than local deer. (Museum of the American West, Autry National Center, Los Angeles; 93.236.1.)

Officers might keep hounds to accompany them in the pursuit of game or while off duty to relax on the veranda of one of the Fort Bowie officers' quarters. (Museum of the American West, Autry National Center, Los Angeles; 93.236.1.)

Fort Grant, established in 1873 near a previous post of the same name that honored Ulysses Grant, was garrisoned by various infantry and cavalry units and came to be considered one of the most desirable military reservations in Arizona. Medical personnel also staffed the post hospital, which is seen here. (Sharlot Hall Museum.)

Maintaining a supply of uniforms and insignia was the duty of quartermaster personnel who, at Fort Grant, had a rather sophisticated storage system for such purposes. (National Archives.)

Troopers stand their post at Fort Grant's stone guardhouse where the interior clock kept the official time for the post, although that system was not without its problems. (Sharlot Hall Museum.)

Supposedly, Capt. William H. Brown of the 5th U.S. Cavalry had "the idea of constructing one large building" for the bachelor officers, and the government authorized $10,000 for the project, but it cost four times that amount. According to the post surgeon's son Harold Corbusier, this structure was nicknamed "Brown's Folly" because it was a "large, ugly stone structure, and the first one built at the post." (Arizona Historical Society.)

The evening gun at Fort Grant, Arizona, in the 1880s was a Model 1840 mountain howitzer. While a functional artillery piece, the howitzer also was fired as the garrison lowered the national colors to conclude the military day. (Sharlot Hall Museum.)

The butcher shop at Fort Grant, while not the model of sanitation, provided relatively inexpensive fresh meat for those who wished to purchase beef from this source. According to Harold Corbusier, whose father was the post doctor during the 1880s, this facility provided "big juicy steaks, roasts, price nine cents a pound. And the other choice bits were always included free of charge! Little Mother knew full well the value of liver, kidney, sweetbread, brains, etc. and all these for nothing!" (Sharlot Hall Museum.)

When not serving in the guardhouse, prisoners from Fort Grant might be assigned to saw firewood while a trooper supervised the punishment detail. The post's target range and the Graham Mountains are seen in the background. (U.S. Army Military History Institute.)

Fort Grant military prisoners use an army dump cart as they clean up a portion of the post while being overseen by a guard wearing a summer helmet. (Sharlot Hall Museum.)

Uniformity was not the order of the day, whether in garrison or in the field, for troops stationed in Arizona during the early 1880s, as indicated by these men from the 6th U.S. Cavalry. Supply challenges and the faraway locale of posts, such as Fort Grant, contributed to this situation. (National Archives.)

Despite a fairly sophisticated irrigation system at Fort Grant, water wagons were still required to bring potable water to the quarters. (Sharlot Hall Museum.)

In contrast to the drudgery of work detail, troopers form rank in dress helmets topped with gala yellow horsetail plumes for dress parade with the enlisted barracks in the background at Fort

Grant. (National Archives.)

Founded in 1877, Fort Huachuca was a key assembly point for troops who could guard the border or mobilize for field duty near traditional routes taken by the Apaches to and from Mexico. (U.S. Army Military History Institute.)

During the 1880s at Fort Huachuca, the 4th U.S. Cavalry, Troop C, lived in an adobe barrack that was not as substantial as the wooden ones housing their comrades. The latter structures still stand, while this one of mud brick was demolished in 1964. (Fort Huachuca Museum.)

Wooden barracks, seen here under construction in the 1880s, were an improvement over the ones of adobe at Fort Huachuca. They remain standing to this day. (Fort Huachuca Museum.)

Water was the lifeblood of a post, and Fort Huachuca's reservoir was vital to sustaining that garrison. (Arizona Historical Society.)

Officers and family members picnic at Garden Canyon, an oasis near Fort Huachuca that provided a respite from the daily garrison routine. (Museum of the American West, Autry National Center, Los Angeles; 93.236.1.)

Stables played an important part of Fort Huachuca's infrastructure, as they did at other installations around the territory. (Fort Huachuca Museum.)

Stables not only protected cavalry mounts from the elements but also sheltered draft animals and their harnesses for wagons, ambulances, and other army vehicles. (Fort Huachuca Museum.)

By the late 1800s, Fort Huachuca's officers' quarters were comfortable homes for their inhabitants. (Capt. Alexander Macomb, USN [Ret.], Fort Huachuca Museum.)

Mrs. Batchelor's Parlor.

The arrival of the railroad in southern Arizona during the 1880s meant officers could furnish their quarters with any luxury they could afford. (Leavell Collection, Fort Huachuca Museum.)

Fort Huachuca remained active even at the conclusion of the so-called Indian Wars when men, such as Private Suthard (left) and Corporal Page of the 14th U.S. Cavalry, served there in the early 1900s. (Fort Huachuca Museum.)

Fort Huachuca's officers' club in the 1920s provided meals, drink, and fellowship. Today the structure is part of the post's museum complex. (Fort Huachuca Museum.)

Surgeon Joseph Girard captured the landscape around Fort Lowell, outside of Tucson, the territory's major civilian center of political and economic influence. (Arizona Historical Society.)

Surgeon Girard's quarters at Fort Lowell are shown above as they appeared in 1889, not long before the post would be abandoned. (Arizona Historical Society.)

This view is of Fort Lowell, as seen from the west side, during its last years as an active military installation. (Arizona Historical Society.)

Whether playing a local civilian nine or a visiting team from Fort Huachuca (seen here), baseball was played at Fort Lowell and several other Victorian-era Arizona posts. (Arizona Historical Society.)

Strains of music from the 6th U.S. Cavalry band floated over the parade ground during martial ceremonies and as entertainment for members of the garrison and locals alike at Fort Lowell. (Arizona Historical Society.)

This post was originally known as Camp McDowell when it was established by elements of the 1st California Volunteer Cavalry on September 7, 1865. It is in the vicinity of modern-day Phoenix and remained in operation as a military installation until December 1890. (Sharlot Hall Museum.)

In the late 1860s, Sutler's Store was an earlier version of the post exchange where members of a garrison, such as these men gathered at Fort McDowell, could purchase a limited variety of goods and some luxuries. (Arizona Historical Society.)

The Gatling gun was an early form of a rapid-fire weapon and predecessor to the machine gun. Men of the 6th U.S. Cavalry, Company I, at Fort McDowell pose with this seldom-deployed piece of technology that dated to the Civil War era. (Sharlot Hall Museum.)

This May Day picnic held in 1878 by officers of the 8th U.S. Infantry and some of their family members at Fort McDowell, Arizona, was typical of the type of outing enjoyed at many frontier forts. (Sharlot Hall Museum.)

A primitive tent camp at Camp San Carlos was established to maintain order at the nearby reservation that bore the same name. (National Archives.)

Although peace had come to Arizona Territory when this photograph was taken at Camp San Carlos during the early 1890s, troopers of the 7th U.S. Cavalry still practiced using their mounts for protection as they fired their carbines. By this time, the installation had taken on a more permanent status. (National Archives.)

Enlisted men of 1st U.S. Cavalry, Troop C, took turns preparing meals for their "bunkies" in the mess hall kitchen at Camp San Carlos. (U.S. Cavalry Museum, Fort Riley.)

Established in 1876 some 6 miles east of old Camp Goodwin, Fort Thomas was situated near the San Carlos Agency to control Native Americans on that reservation. The post was named in honor of Lorenzo Thomas, adjutant general of the U.S. Army during the Civil War. (U.S. Army Military History Institute.)

Fort Yuma, on the west side of the Colorado River, was linked closely with the outposts of Arizona Territory. An amateur artist of the 1850s captured the look of the post during its early days. (Arizona Historical Society.)

This is the parade ground at Fort Yuma as it appeared around 1880. (Arizona Historical Society.)

This is Fort Yuma as seen from the east around 1875. (Arizona Historical Society.)

TROOP STREET, CAMP HARRY J. JONES.   DOUGLAS, ARIZ.

Camp Harry J. Jones (named for a corporal killed in a 1915 raid by Pancho Villa's forces) was located near Douglas and began as a "sea of canvas," as future World War II general Lucian Truscott described the original tent encampment. (George M. Langellier Jr.)

CANTONMENTS, CAMP HARRY J. JONES.   DOUGLAS, ARIZ.

Soon Camp Jones blossomed. The post had 15 streets, and wooden barracks stood along the tent city. The troops were stationed there to maintain order along the troubled border with Mexico. (George M. Langellier Jr.)

BASE HOSPITAL, CAMP HARRY J. JONES.   DOUGLAS, ARIZ.

Seen here is a hospital to treat the sick. (George M. Langellier Jr.)

ARMY Y. M. C. A., CAMP HARRY J. JONES.   DOUGLAS, ARIZ.

The men could find respite from duties at Camp Jones at the YMCA. (George M. Langellier Jr.)

REGIMENTAL BAND CONCERT, CAMP HARRY J. JONES.   DOUGLAS, ARIZ.

Regimental bands provided entertainment and played for military formations at Camp Jones. (George M. Langellier Jr.)

Men of the 25th U.S. Infantry left the relative comforts of Fort Huachuca to keep watch at the border of Nogales where they lived in Camp Stephen D. Little. (George M. Langellier Jr.)

Two

ARMY FAMILIES

Army regulations provided only limited official recognition for family members, including wives, daughters, sons, and others who accompanied officers and enlisted men. The former group who followed the guidon—as Elizabeth Custer described the women and children who shared the privations of duty at remote military installations—were the spouses of officers. They often came from educated and well-to-do families. Consequently, their days at these often desolate outposts were, as one army wife phrased it, "glittering misery."

Women who married enlisted men almost always were from impoverished backgrounds and crammed into "soapsuds row" or other mean dwellings at a post. Some of them became laundresses, the only women (in addition to the occasional hospital matron) who were officially sanctioned by the army. Taking on positions as domestics brought in supplemental funding that was needed given the limited pay from the military to their soldier husbands.

In 1907, Ellen Biddle published a memoir detailing her days in the West as the wife of James Biddle, a 6th U.S. Cavalry officer who reported to Arizona in 1876. (*Reminiscences of A Soldier's Wife.*)

Yours Sincerely Martha Summerhayes

Martha Summerhayes lived in Arizona Territory with her army husband. Despite the challenges, she also set down her story in a 1908 book about her days with her beloved Jack, an 8th U.S. Infantry officer. (*Vanished Arizona.*)

Just before her 24th birthday, Carrie McGavock would marry Samuel Whitside in Nashville, Tennessee. Nearly a decade later, her husband would report to Arizona where, among his other duties, he established Fort Huachuca. (Fort Huachuca Museum.)

The 6th U.S. Cavalry lieutenant Louis A. Craig's children, Malin and Helen (left), were among the youngsters who called such garrisons as Fort Bowie and Fort Huachuca home. Craig's daughter was the first child to be born at the latter post, and his son would follow in his father's footsteps and become a cavalry officer. (Fort Huachuca Museum.)

The Graham Mountains offered an escape for fortunate members of the Fort Grant garrison during the summer, including Anson Mills Jr., Willie Corbusier, and Constance Mills. The man standing in front of the fourth tent is "Long Jim" Cook, and seated to the right is a former trooper turned hunter/guide by the name of Montgomery. (Arizona Historical Society.)

Children of Anson Mills (the post commander) and Dr. Corbusier fall into line as they pretend they are army troopers at Fort Grant during the 1880s. Anson Mills Jr. (far left) is joined by Constance Mills (center) and Willie Corbusier (second from right). (*My Story*.)

Reservoir Canyon, which was a major source of water for Fort Grant, also was the site of an 1887 picnic for the family of post surgeon William Corbusier and some of their fellow inhabitants of the fort. (Arizona Historical Society.)

The water from the reservoir fed Lake Constance on Fort Grant's parade ground, where bathers from the families of Dr. Corbusier and Major Mills canoe and swim. (Arizona Historical Society.)

Post surgeon William Corbusier and his family lived in these adobe quarters at Fort Grant, which served as a backdrop for a January 1888 photograph of the household, including Dr. and Mrs.

Corbusier (seated on chair on the veranda), their five sons. (Arizona Historical Society.)

The environs of Fort Thomas in 1881 offered a setting for picnicking with the family of Anson Mills (second from left) and C. D. Viele (back right, behind his wife) and fellow officers R. D. Reed and H. D. Whipple. (Arizona Historical Society.)

Captain Macomb's family is about to drive away from their Fort Huachuca quarters to enjoy a buggy ride. (Capt. Alexander Macomb, USN [Ret.] Collection, Fort Huachuca Museum.)

Delighted officers and their families are seen here at a 1903 formal ball held at the Fort Huachuca recreation hall. (Capt. Alexander Macomb, USN [Ret.] Collection, Fort Huachuca Museum.)

During World War I, Capt. Frederick Ryder of the 10th U.S. Cavalry evidently engaged a family member of one of the African American troops at Fort Huachuca to assist with the care of a baby. (F. H. L. Ryder Collection, Fort Huachuca Museum.)

Esther Buchanan Smith served as Fort Huachuca's postmistress from 1920 to 1921. She had arrived at the post nearly a dozen years before and lived there with her aunt, whom she succeeded in overseeing the garrison's mail. (Esther Buchanan Smith Collection, Fort Huachuca Museum.)

Three

FIELD OPERATIONS

While life in Arizona garrisons was not always exciting, the requirement to take to the field for training or on campaign provided a change of pace; however, this break in monotony had its price. Whether setting out in pursuit of native people who came to be known as Apaches, striking the trail for other Indian groups, or protecting the often volatile international boundary, the cavalry, infantry, occasionally artillery, and other branches faced hardships, injury, and even death. The elements could be brutal, with alternating blazing heat and freezing cold. Water often was scarce, and rations were of poor quality or sometimes scant.

The 8th U.S. Cavalry, Troop I, reports to Arizona in 1867. They were assigned to Fort Whipple and later to Fort McDowell. The troopers were among the first post–Civil War horse soldiers to report to the territory. (Kansas State Historical Society, Topeka.)

Officers and men of the 8th U.S. Infantry are joined temporarily by some of nearby Fort McDowell's ladies, who have come to visit the soldiers where they could develop experience for the field. (National Archives.)

The 1876 pattern campaign hat featured miniature fan blades in the crown to cool the wearer, in theory.

Sgt. Emil Pauly, standing in the center of this 1884 picture taken near Bisbee, is joined by other members of 4th U.S. Cavalry, Troop I, and Indian scouts who served in the field. (Fort Huachuca Museum.)

Swedish native Neil Erickson (center) and two other enlisted men from the 4th U.S. Cavalry, Troop E, are decked out for the field with a combination of army issue and privately purchased items for their campaign kits. At 27 years old, Erickson became his troop's first sergeant. After

an honorable discharge in late 1886, he remained in Arizona and started a ranch near today's Chiricahua National Monument and Fort Bowie. (National Park Service.)

The 6th U.S. Cavalry, Troop A, had been stationed at Camp San Carlos and Fort Apache, but by 1885, they would leave humdrum garrison routine to rough it on the Mexican border. (National Archives.)

From left to right, Indian scouts Apache Kid and Slim Jim stand with Sergeant Hannikin and civilian employee Bob Tribolett at Mudsprings, 18 miles north of Douglas, Arizona. (Fort Huachuca Museum.)

Transporting the injured, sick, or wounded in the field required considerable ingenuity given the rugged terrain in Arizona and the distances between medical facilities. (Library of Congress.)

Carrying water and other vital supplies into the field posed a problem that usually was addressed by employing pack mules and civilian packers sometimes assisted by troops. (Library of Congress.)

Photo by FLY.

Geronimo (seated third from the left in a calico bandana) meets with Gen. George Crook (wearing his signature sun helmet second from right) to discuss his return to U.S. territory after the Apache leader's years of raiding there and in Mexico. (National Archives.)

In 1886, Gen. George Crook (seated in center wearing pith helmet) is joined in the first row by members of his staff and others including (fifth from left, in white shirt) Tom Horn, Tucson's mayor (seventh from left), Charles M. Strauss (10th from left), Lt. William Shipp (12th from left),

Capt. John Bourke (14th from left, with large white hat, dark shirt, and suspenders), and civilian Al Sieber who was chief of scouts. Tom Horn is sitting fifth from the left in the white shirt. (Fort Huachuca Museum.)

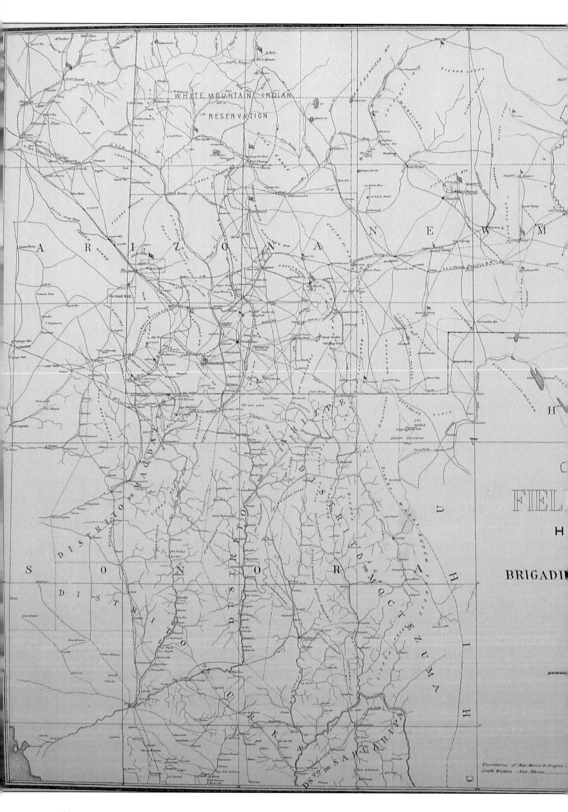

E MAP
of the

PERATIONS

against

RICAHUA INDIANS

the date of their Surrender September 4th 1886.

Drawn by Direction of

NELSON A. MILES

Department of Arizona
office of

E.J. SPENCER.
f Engineers.
R OF THE DEPARTMENT.

Top. Assistant.
1st Cavalry

END

Rivers Roads and Trails practicable.
for Wagons
Trails practicable for Pack mules
International Boundary
Fixed territorial boundaries
and Boundaries of Indian Military
Reservations
On U.S. Limits of Districts of
observation under command of
senior officers Chosen
On Mount Prohibitive Limits

Authorities

South Western Division .... Dr. E.J. Spencer
Official Map of the State of Sonora .... R.H. Marhael

Nelson Miles depended less on Indian scouts than he did on the British-inspired heliograph, a device that used mirrors for line-of-sight communication. A widespread system of heliograph stations ultimately was established throughout much of the Southwest to supplement mounted couriers and telegraph lines, the latter communication network being rather restricted and traditionally tied to railroad lines. The heliograph remained in use for several years after Native American campaigning ended. (George M. Langellier Jr.)

63

Heliograph Station No. 3, Bowie District, Arizona, is shown above as it appeared in 1890. From left to right are Lt. A. M. Fuller, Cpl. Charles Swope, Pvts. Thomas Harvey and W. H. Bowker,

Sgt. William Wade, and Pvts. Charles Laing, F. W. Allen, Thomas Persee, and Adolph Miller. (National Archives.)

Pvt. William Kane (standing) and a fellow trooper from the 4th U.S. Cavalry are armed with experimental bolt-action carbines ready for the field in 1886. (Fort Huachuca Museum.)

Troopers of the 6th U.S. Cavalry are mounted and ready to ride against Geronimo and his band that eluded many would-be captors in the 1870s and 1880s. (National Archives.)

Not all excursions into the field were related to combat. During late 1887 and early 1888, Lt. Edward Casey set out to chart then little-known areas of Arizona and New Mexico, such as Baker's Peak in the former territory. Note the oversized canteens that were larger than standard army issue and developed for desert use. (National Archives.)

Maintaining combat readiness brought men of the 24th U.S. Infantry to a training camp at Garden Canyon outside Fort Huachuca in 1894. (C. B. Ebert Collection, Fort Huachuca Museum.)

Occasional fighting continued even after Geronimo's departure from Arizona, such as this minor

engagement in 1895 at Nippurs, 35 miles southwest of Bowie. (National Archives.)

Orlando Troxel was the youthful commander for the 10th U.S. Cavalry, Troop D, at Naco, during border troubles in 1915. (Fort Huachuca Museum.)

National guardsmen of the 1st Arizona Infantry were called out in 1915 as reinforcements to protect the troubled border with its neighbor to the south. They were assigned to Naco. (Paul Ballinger Collection, Fort Huachuca Museum.)

The need to protect the border between the United States and Mexico brought out national guardsmen from California to supplement the regular army garrison at Fort Huachuca. (Fort Huachuca Museum.)

Although new technologies had been developed, Victorian-style heliographs remained in use in 1916 along the Mexican border. (Fort Huachuca Museum.)

Instead of shipping out to the battlefields of Europe, some of Lt. Chuck Close's World War I service was spent at Arivaca, Arizona, in 1918. (F. H. L. Ryder Collection, Fort Huachuca Museum.)

Troops from Fort Huachuca were deployed to Nogales as artillerymen at Camp Stephen D. Little. (George M. Langellier Jr.)

Four

COMMANDERS

Prior to 1861, the few officers posted to what was to become Arizona Territory typically had attended West Point. With the coming of war between the North and South, this cadre left to serve either in the blue or the gray. After that conflict concluded, many of the officers posted to Arizona were Union veterans. Some came from civilian life and others were graduates of the U.S. Military Academy. As the decades passed, once again the majority of those who held commissions did so because of West Point training. Some of these young men went on to distinguished careers during World War I, and in some instances World War II. Whether they had prior service or were newly commissioned cadets, nothing in their past experience prepared them for the duty that faced them.

They led a small force that typically shared their inexperience. Their subordinates differed from the men who wore shoulder straps in that the majority of them had little education and came from meager means. A significant percent were from abroad, with large numbers of sons of Irish and Germans and a smattering of English, Italian, French, and Canadian men filling the ranks. There also were many among the rank and file who were born in the United States. Whether from big cities or small farming communities, they served for little reward, with the monthly pay starting at $13 for a private for most of the decades between the late 1860s and into the early 20th century. The paltry pay contributed to a high desertion rate, yet officers and men managed to do their duty in a place that was as foreign to them as the moon.

Charles Veil's Civil War record led to his promotion from the ranks. He received a commission after Gettysburg, as indicated by his epaulettes bearing the silver bars of a captain. In 1866, Veil reported to Arizona with 1st U.S. Cavalry, Company C. Soon he and his men established Camp Lowell in Tucson. For generations, family members have preserved artifacts from his military career. (Fred Veil.)

Lt. Otto Hein of the 1st U.S. Cavalry set down his recollections about military life, including posting to Arizona in the early 1870s in a book titled *Memories of Long Ago*. (National Archives.)

West Point graduate Oliver Otis Howard became a general during the Civil War. When peace came, he was named the chief commissioner of the Freedman's Bureau, under the auspices of which he founded Howard University in Washington, D.C., in 1867. He then was posted to Arizona where he led the campaign against Cochise's band. Howard was a major player in efforts of Ulysses S. Grant's administration to bring peace to the troubled territory. (U.S. Army Military History Institute.)

English-born 1st Lt. Jonathan Sladen of the 14th U.S. Infantry cast off any semblance of martial attire when he prepared for field duty in Arizona during 1872. In that year, he served with General Howard and met with notable Chiricahua leader Cochise to seek a peace treaty. Prior to service in Arizona, Sladen's heroism during the Civil War would be recognized with a Medal of Honor. (U.S. Army Military History Institute.)

Gen. George Crook spent much of his long military career in the West, starting in California. After fighting Confederate guerrillas during the Civil War, he came west again. One of Crook's biographers asserted the general "was sincerely interested in the welfare of the Indians and in justice to red and white alike; he was intrepid, of generally noble sentiments and his influence is felt to the present day in Indian-white relations." (Fort Huachuca Museum.)

Maj. Gen. Orlando Willcox commanded the Department of Arizona from 1878 to 1882 but is best remembered because of a town in the state that bears his name. (Fort Huachuca Museum.)

After the attack on Fort Sumter in South Carolina, Nelson Appleton Miles, a self-educated Boston grocery clerk, joined the Union cause. This unlikely candidate for military life proved his courage in numerous battles and rose rapidly through the ranks, receiving four wounds and being recognized for valor with a Medal of Honor. In the postwar era, he served on the Great Plains and later replaced Crook in Arizona during the final campaign against Geronimo. (National Archives.)

Benjamin Grierson served as colonel of the 10th U.S. Cavalry for over two decades, including several years after the regiment arrived in Arizona in 1885. (National Archives.)

Civil War Medal of Honor recipient Eugene Carr served in Arizona as lieutenant colonel of the 5th U.S. Cavalry and returned to the territory as colonel of the 6th U.S. Cavalry. He was in charge at Cibecue, which was a major clash that involved a rare occasion when one of the garrisons was besieged as in a motion picture plot. (National Archives.)

Capt. Emmet Crawford of the 3rd U.S. Cavalry performed vigorously in Arizona and Mexico against Apaches. During January 1885, on one of his forays trailing Geronimo, he received a mortal wound from Mexican irregular troops. (National Archives.)

With the conclusion of George Crook's first assignment to Arizona, August V. Kautz (center of photograph with his fellow 8th U.S. Infantry officers) arrived to assume command of the army troops in the territory. As with many of his contemporaries, he was a Civil War veteran and, as indicated by the two stars on his collar, had held the grade of major general of volunteers. Although an able administrator, Kautz was not well liked by many influential citizens in the southern part of the territory. (U.S. Army Military History Institute.)

Lt. Charles Gatewood served vigorously under both Crook and Miles. His efforts to capture Geronimo were overshadowed by others who may not have contributed as much to the Geronimo campaign as he did. (National Archives.)

This is a 4th U.S. Cavalry officer's dress helmet with a yellow buffalo hair plume, which was regulation from 1881 through 1903. (George M. Langellier Jr.)

Officers also wore knots with their regimental number of branch insignia when in full dress uniform, such as this example for a first lieutenant of the 5th U.S. Cavalry. (George M. Langellier Jr.)

George Crook likewise depended on Adna Chaffee of the 6th U.S. Cavalry, who became a general and played an important command role during the 1900 relief expedition to Perking, China. (George M. Langellier Jr.)

Henry Lawton, 4th U.S. Cavalry officer, would receive considerable credit for bringing an end to hostilities with Geronimo's band, which would help him rise from captain to brigadier general by the time of the war with Spain. (Fort Huachuca Museum.)

Standing some 6 feet in height, Capt. George Anderson (the tall man to the right in front of his men) was rather large for a mounted officer. He came to Arizona in 1875 and, after reporting to San Carlos, transferred to become an aide to August Kautz. He rose over the decades to retire as a brigadier general. One of his assignments after Arizona was as superintendent of Yellowstone National Park. (Arizona Historical Society.)

Wirt Davis began his military career as an enlisted man before the Civil War won him a commission with the 4th U.S. Cavalry. By 1884, he served with his regiment in Arizona, including Forts Lowell, Bowie, and Huachuca, before being promoted to major and transferring from the territory. (U.S. Army Military History Institute.)

From 1875 to 1881, William Baird served with the 6th U.S. Cavalry in Arizona and thereafter compiled a distinguished record. (Frontier Army Museum, Fort Leavenworth.)

William A. Thompson of the 4th U.S. Cavalry was a captain when he arrived for duty at Fort Bowie in 1884 in command of Troop G. After that, he spent most of the next three years on active campaign against the Apaches. (National Archives.)

Poor health caused John W. Martin to resign from West Point, but when his medical situation improved, he secured a commission with the 4th U.S. Cavalry. He spent his early years in Texas and, in 1885, joined his regiment in Arizona, where he remained on duty until a heart condition ultimately led to his retirement. (National Archives.)

Soon after graduation in 1877 from the U.S. Military Academy, Stephen Mills (center) set aside his cadet gray and adopted civilian frontier garb. He would be placed in command of an Indian scout detachment at Fort Thomas and also served at Fort Huachuca. Much of his time in Arizona was spent in the field until he went east in charge of the Chiricahua prisoners of war who were sent to Florida in 1886. (U.S. Army Military History Institute.)

Although he graduated last in his class from West Point, Powhattan Clarke demonstrated his grit in combat and received a Medal of Honor for rescuing one of his 10th U.S. Cavalry troopers during a tense firefight with Apaches in the mid-1880s. He became friends with Frederic Remington, who produced this jaunty rendering of the young Virginia-born officer. (George M. Langellier Jr.)

Five

BUFFALO SOLDIERS

Many African Americans made great sacrifices while fighting for freedom in the Civil War that tore the United States asunder between 1861 and 1865. Nearly 180,000 blacks served the Union cause in uniform during that conflict. In 1866, shortly after the end of this national tragedy, African Americans, for the first time, were allowed to enlist in the regular army during peacetime. These black regulars would be posted to the American West, but it wasn't until spring 1885 that black troops reported for duty in today's Arizona. In that year, the 10th U.S. Cavalry regiment moved from the Department of Texas to the Department of Arizona, marching along the Southern Pacific Railroad. The regiment would arrive at Bowie, where the troops separated to go to their several stations, including Fort Whipple outside of Prescott, Fort Apache, Fort Thomas, Fort Grant, and Fort Verde. Over the decades, the 10th Cavalry and other regiments of these so-called "buffalo soldiers" (a term used by artist Frederic Remington in the 1880s, although the origin of the nickname is debated) arrived and served at many Arizona posts, but through World War II, their main home came to be Fort Huachuca.

Albert F. Kovarik

FORT GRANT,
ARIZONA.

An unidentified private of the 10th U.S. Cavalry had his portrait taken at Fort Grant in the late 1880s, possibly by an itinerant photographer. (George M. Langellier Jr.)

The 10th U.S. Cavalry, Troop G, guards Native American prisoners being brought to trial in Tucson. (National Archives.)

89085

Cpl. Isaiah Mays of the 24th U.S. Infantry was wounded while on escort duty with a military paymaster. He and another enlisted man from the detail would be recognized for bravery and presented Medals of Honor. (Library of Congress.)

Isaiah Mays would die with meager means and be buried in a forgotten grave at the Arizona State Hospital after his death in 1925. Ultimately his remains would be transferred to a grave in Arlington National Cemetery in keeping with his status as a Medal of Honor recipient. (George M. Langellier Jr.)

89

The 25th U.S. Infantry, Company H, strides out with pride as they depart Fort Huachuca in 1899 to embark for the Philippines. The regiment also had served in Cuba during the prior year. (National Archives.)

Bandsmen of the 25th U.S. Infantry lived in Spartan barracks at Fort Huachuca. The open bay arrangement left little privacy. (National Archives.)

Border unrest brought 10th U.S. Cavalry, Troop D, to Naco just before the United States entered World War I. (Fort Huachuca Museum.)

Barrack life in the early 20th century permitted black cavalry troopers free time that they could occupy with a wide variety of diversions, including shooting dice. (Markel Collection, Fort Huachuca Museum.)

Seen here in 1915, Charles H. Grierson, a captain at Fort Huachuca, stands on the steps of his quarters with family members and their dog. His father also had been a cavalry officer and was the 10th U.S. Cavalry's first regimental commander when the unit was formed in 1866. Both the Griersons were typical of the officers who commanded the regiment in that nearly all were white men. (Charles H. Grierson Collection, Fort Huachuca Museum.)

Men of the 10th U.S. Cavalry had to be prepared for duty away from Fort Huachuca. By 1918, they had field kitchens to improve the rations issued when serving away from the post. (Markel Collection, Fort Huachuca Museum.)

The men resorted to more primitive means to prepare food in the field, as these soldiers of 10th U.S. Cavalry, Troop E, and civilian mule packers demonstrate at Tucscoso Canyon in 1918. (F.H.L. Ryder Collection, Fort Huachuca Museum.)

First Sergeant Thomas Jordan, 10th U.S. Cavalry, Troop F, appears atop his well-groomed mount while at the Nogales pistol range in April 1919. The sergeant was typical of many African American troopers in his regiment in that he was a long-serving soldier. At the time this snapshot was taken, he had spent 20 years with the troops. Many African American soldiers made a career of the military in the decades after the Civil War, as opportunities in the civilian sector were limited and Jim Crow was the law of the land. (Fort Huachuca Museum.)

In 1921, troopers of the 10th U.S. Cavalry gather on Fort Huachuca's parade ground. Even in peacetime, these African American horse soldiers had to keep their equestrian skills at top levels of proficiency. The row of quarters in the background stands today as mute witness to bygone days when the hoofbeats of cavalry mounts echoed across the post. (Fort Huachuca Museum.)

Sports like baseball kept men of the 10th U.S. Cavalry fit and offered recreation. In this image, men of Troop I gather to have their picture taken for claiming the honor of winning the regimental championship in 1921. (Fort Huachuca Museum.)

Another change of pace occurred at Fort Huachuca in 1925 when Fox Studios came to the post and used men of the 10th U.S. Cavalry and Apache Indian scouts as extras for a film titled *The Golden Strain*. (U.S. Army Military History Institute.)

In 1928, soldiers from 25th U.S. Infantry, Company M, engage in bayonet practice outside their Fort Huachuca barracks. (Fort Huachuca Museum.)

During the Civil War, 24th U.S. Infantry chaplain Allen Allensworth escaped the yoke of slavery. After that conflict, he studied theology and was ordained. He would join his regiment where he provided spiritual and educational support to his soldier flock. (National Archives.)

Chaplain Louis A. Carter rose to the rank of lieutenant colonel. He served with the 25th U.S. Infantry at Camp Stephen D. Little in Nogales during the 1920s and Fort Huachuca in the 1930s. Like Chaplain Allensworth, he was a proponent of educational opportunities for enlisted men. (Fort Huachuca Museum.)

The 25th U.S. Infantry guard was manned by distinguished enlisted men in 1933. They are at attention for a visit from General of the Armies of the United States John "Black Jack" Pershing at Fort Huachuca. Pershing's nickname was derived from his service commanding African American troopers in the late 19th century. (Fort Huachuca Museum.)

In another 1933 photograph, the 25th U.S. Infantry band stands at attention and ready to play. (U.S. Army Military History Institute.)

This is a group portrait of members at the headquarters of the 25th U.S. Infantry and noncommissioned officers of the regiment's second battalion during the 1930s. (U.S. Army Military History Institute.)

Men of the 25th U.S. Infantry, Company F, take a time-out for chow and line up with mess kits in hand. (Fort Huachuca Museum.)

The 93rd Division was reactivated at Fort Huachuca on May 15, 1942. Soon the troops began to learn about the hazards of military service where even cactus could be an enemy. Sgt. William Wilson comes to the aid of Pvt. Thurman Brownlee. (Fort Huachuca Museum.)

Fort Huachuca's honor guard turns out on May 19, 1942. (U.S. Army Military History Institute.)

This is one of the barracks occupied by men of the 93rd Division in 1943. These humble quarters varied little from their counterparts in the late 19th century. (U.S. Army Military History Institute.)

World War II resulted in horses being replaced by steel steeds at Fort Huachuca. (U.S. Army Military History Institute.)

Regimental bands gave way to divisional bands during World War II, as in the case of the martial musicians of the 93rd Division at Fort Huachuca. (U.S. Army Military History Institute.)

Lucille Mayo (left) and Ruth Wade of the Women's Army Corps (WAC) put their skills to the test at the Fort Huachuca motor pool to do their bit for the war effort. (Fort Huachuca Museum.)

In addition to WACs, African American U.S. Army nurses served at the fort. (Fort Huachuca Museum.)

Count cadence, men! Troops of the 93rd Division drill with their M-1 Garand rifles. (Fort Huachuca Museum.)

Gen. George Marshall found time to inspect a mess hall where elements of the 92nd division dined. (Fort Huachuca Museum.)

Gen. George Marshall, U.S. Army Chief of Staff, (left) was joined by other high-ranking officers to review the 92nd Infantry Division in 1943. The division was constituted of African American enlisted men but commanded in the main by white officers in a segregated army that remained government policy until 1948. (Fort Huachuca Museum.)

Six

INDIAN SCOUTS

In 1866, U.S. Congress officially authorized the enlistment of Indian scouts. These men came from many Native American groups and served under white officers or other non-Indian leaders. Brigadier George Crook was an especially active proponent for the deployment of Indian scouts in the Southwest. During an interview with one newspaper correspondent, Crook revealed his philosophy about the employment of scouts: "To polish a diamond, there is nothing like its own diamond dust; the same with these fellows. Nothing breaks them up like running their own people against them."

Their reasons for service were complex and varied. Some enlisted for prestige, the ability to maintain warrior traditions, or to support their families financially (enlistments were for six months). Fighting traditional enemies or revenge sometimes entered into the picture. Regardless of the motives and except for a few rare occasions, such as a mutiny of the scouts in the early 1880s at Cibecue during a religious revival among some of those living on the reservation near Fort Apache, their service usually was honorable and, in many cases, valiant.

Most Indian scouts in Arizona Territory served faithfully, such as Slim Jim on the right, although a few mutinied or went astray, such as Eke-be-nadel (middle), who was later known as "The Apache Kid." (Fort Huachuca Museum.)

Apache scouts at Fort Huachuca in 1879 are seen with an army sergeant named Edward Murphy standing on the left. (Fort Huachuca Museum.)

Cushets, who was nicknamed "Tom," was a member of the White Mountain Apaches (so-called because of their traditional territory in the White Mountains). He was among the mutinous scouts at Cibecue. (National Archives.)

Called "Dutchy" by the whites because of his fair coloring, this Chiricahua was a mainstay as a scout with Lt. Britton Davis. Ultimately he abandoned military service to join Geronimo and would be transported to Florida as a prisoner of war. (National Archives.)

The whites nicknamed Tso-ay "Peaches" because of his fair, smooth skin. After being captured by the army while raiding, he agreed to become a scout. Despite loyal service, he would be exiled to Florida with Geronimo and others. (National Archives.)

Capt. Emmet Crawford's Apache scouts were with him in 1886 when he was killed by Mexican forces in the Sierra Madres. (National Archives.)

These Apaches at right were members of the B Company of Indian scouts. (National Archives.)

Lt. Marion Maus, in a rather rakish musketeer-style nonregulation campaign hat, takes to the field with some of the Apache scouts under his command during the 1880s. (Fort Huachuca Museum.)

Apache scouts typically combined army issue, such as the sergeant in a regulation blouse on the left, with traditional garb of their people. (National Archives.)

Capt. John Bourke, Crook's aide, indicated that "The longer we knew Apache scouts, the better we liked them. They were wilder and more suspicious than the Pimas and Maricopas, but far more reliable, and endowed with a greater amount of courage and daring. I have never known an officer whose experience entitled his opinion to the slightest consideration, who did not believe as I do on this subject." Apache scouts Alchesay (right) and Dutchy (left) both embodied the captain's description. The men flank Brigadier General Crook, who is wearing his trademark summer helmet and is astride one of his favorite mules, which he named Apache. (National Archives.)

"Cut-Mouth Mose" (seated in the center) was first sergeant of Company A. During the fighting at Cibecue, he remained steadfast to his oath as a scout and fought. (National Archives.)

During the early 1890s, Apaches were assigned to 10th U.S. Infantry, Company I, at Fort Bowie as a short-lived experiment to add all-Indian companies to many of the U.S. Army's cavalry and infantry regiments as regular soldiers rather than as scouts. The concept was soon abandoned. (Museum of the American West, Autry National Center, Los Angeles; 93.236.1.)

Mike Burns's family would be killed by forces from the U.S. Army during the early 1870s. Nonetheless, he would become a scout for the army. He was proud of his service, and years after his last enlistment, he obtained a uniform with the distinctive USS with arrow insignia adopted for Indian scouts in 1890. (Arizona Historical Society.)

Long after the campaigns against Arizona's native peoples had ceased, Indian scouts remained on duty, including Apache Sinew Riley, seen here as he appeared around 1920 or before. (Fort Huachuca Museum.)

During the next decade, Riley posed for the camera again and is seen (left) with his son in this family portrait around 1925. (Fort Huachuca Museum.)

In this staged image taken just prior to the United States's entry into World War II, an Apache scout in 19th-century garb hands a message to radio operators. Their officer is using the most recent electronic communications of that era. (National Archives.)

Indian scouts, from left to right, Sinew Riley, William Major, Kessay Y-32 (a vestige of the days when Apaches received identification numbers), and Antonio Ivan retire at Fort Huachuca on August 28, 1947, signifying the end of an era. (Fort Huachuca Museum.)

Seven

PRESERVING THE PAST

Today Arizona's former frontier outposts are more than a memory. Fortunately several previous posts remain as monuments to a bygone age. These facilities are operated by the National Park Service, the U.S. Army, and other organizations. In almost all cases, modern highways and intestates have replaced the trails once ridden by cavalry troopers more than a century ago, making accessing these museums and historical sites much easier. Even more remote sites are worth the extra effort to travel back to another time where one can experience life as it was in Arizona Territory more than a century ago.

While the echoes of the bugle have ceased over most of southern Arizona's outposts, reminders of those bygone days remain, such as at Fort Lowell in Tucson, where an impressive bronze bugler by Dan Bates greets visitors on the old parade grounds. (Rae Whitley.)

Ruins of Fort Lowell's hospital stand as silent witness to the post's past. (Rae Whitley.)

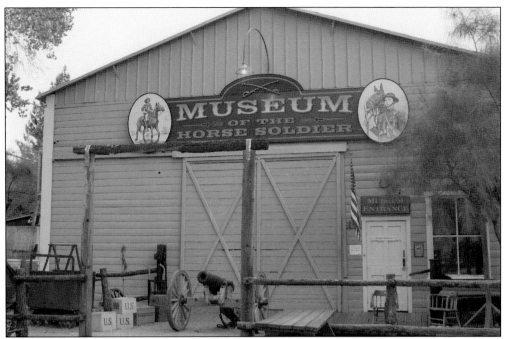

In Tucson, Trail Dust Town visitors also can trace the story of the mounted troops at the Museum of the Horse Soldier. (Ray Whitley.)

The entry gallery to the Museum of the Horse Soldier sets the stage for the visitor's experience. (Ray Whitley.)

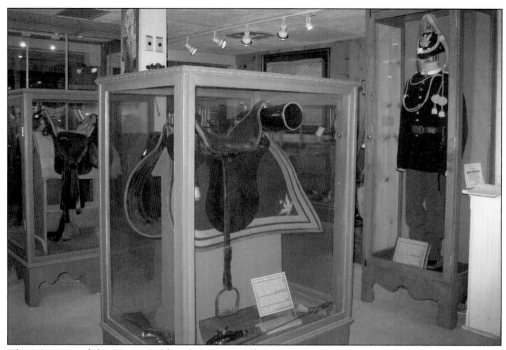

The Museum of the Horse Soldier features saddles, uniforms, weapons, and an impressive array of other artifacts. (Rae Whitley.)

The Museum of the Horse Soldier includes excavated artifacts and information about many of Arizona's 19th- and early-20th-century outposts. (Rae Whitley.)

Early in the 19th century, the machine gun was added to the cavalrymen's arsenal, but this weapon was one of the reasons the era of the horse soldier came to an end. (Rae Whitley.)

Fort Huachuca remains an active U.S. Army military installation generations after the post's founding in 1877. A museum complex traces the story of this significant outpost that has survived from the Indian Wars through the Cold War and on to the present. (Fort Huachuca Museum.)

Among the strengths of the Fort Huachuca Museum are numerous presentations about African American soldiers in southern Arizona. (Fort Huachuca Museum.)

THE BUFFALO SOLDIER
FORT HUACHUCA HONORS THE BUFFALO
SOLDIER, A SYMBOL OF THE PROUD
TRADITION OF THE BLACK FIGHTING MAN
AND REMEMBERS THE PROMINENT ROLE HE
HAS PLAYED IN THE POST'S HISTORY.
3 MARCH 1977
ARTIST IROSE MURRAY

A bronze statue of a buffalo soldier is yet another example of Fort Huachuca's recognition of the role played by African American soldiers. (Fort Huachuca Museum.)

Exhibits related to Indian scouts are featured at the Fort Huachuca Museum, and an impressive bronze statute on the museum grounds captures the spirit of these proud men. (Fort Huachuca Museum.)

Little remains of Fort Bowie's once impressive complex, yet it is well worth a trip off the interstate between Tucson, Arizona, and El Paso, Texas. (U.S. Army Military History Institute.)

Fort Bowie ruins recall the days when Fort Bowie guarded nearby Apache Pass. (Karen Gonzales, Fort Bowie National Historic Site.)

The Fort Bowie Visitors Center provides an overview of the former frontier post. (Karen Gonzales, Fort Bowie National Historic Site.)

A mountain howitzer stands silent guard on the veranda at Fort Bowie. (Karen Gonzales, Fort Bowie National Historic Site.)

This is one of many displays depicting Fort Bowie's past at its visitor center. (Karen Gonzales, Fort Bowie National Historic Site.)

By the 1960s, the parade ground at Fort Yuma appeared very much as it had in an earlier era when the garrison was stationed there. Visitors today will recognize many of the structures from previous military occupation. (National Park Service.)

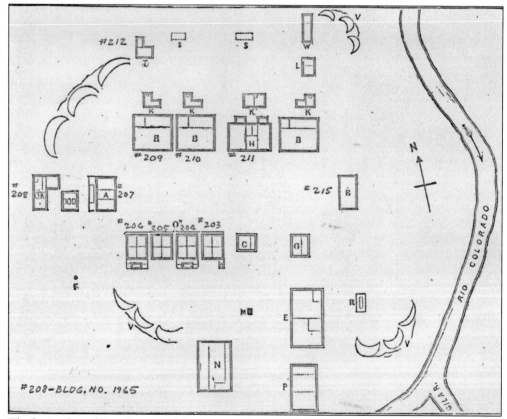

The basic plan of Fort Yuma, California, reveals some of the structures from the period that are still standing.

This post–Civil War plan of the Yuma depot across the river from Fort Yuma in Arizona illustrates the facility that once provided supplies for the posts in the territory.

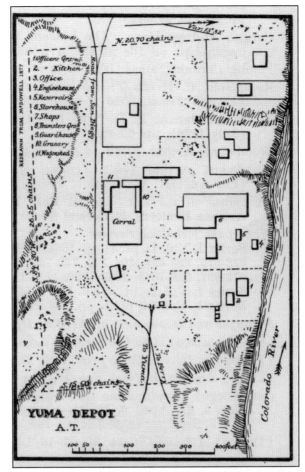

The grounds of the Yuma Depot appear very much as they did during the days when this was an active logistic center for the military in the area. (Yuma Visitors Bureau; photograph by Ann Walker.)

The depot's corral was an important component for maintaining livestock used to conduct local operations or for transfer to other Arizona military establishments. (Yuma Visitors Bureau; photograph by Ann Walker.)

A museum tells the story of the former depot. Exhibits include maps, uniform items, and equipment. (Yuma Visitors Bureau; photograph by Ann Walker.)

BIBLIOGRAPHY

Altshuler, Constance Wynn. *Cavalry Yellow and Infantry Blue: Army Officers in Arizona between 1851 and 1886.* Tucson, AZ: Arizona Historical Society, 1991.

Altshuler, Constance Wynn. *Chains of Command: Arizona and the Army, 1856–1875.* Tucson, AZ: Arizona Historical Society, 1981.

Altshuler, Constance Wynn. *Starting with Defiance: Nineteenth-Century Arizona Military Posts.* Tucson, AZ: Arizona Historical Society, 1983.

Faust, David T., and Kenneth A. Randall. *Life at Post: Fort Lowell, Arizona Territory, 1873–1891, in Smoke Signal. No. 74.* Tucson, AZ: Tucson Corral of the Westerners, 2002.

McChristian, Douglas C. *Fort Bowie, Arizona: Combat Post of the Southwest, 1858–1894.* Norman, OK: University of Oklahoma Press, 2005.

Smith, Cornelius C. *Fort Huachuca: the Story of a Frontier Post.* Washington, D.C.: Department of the Army, 1981.

Stallard, Patricia Y. *Glittering Misery: Dependents of the Indian Fighting Army.* San Rafael, CA: Presidio Press, 1978.

Thrapp, Dan L. *The Conquest of Apacheria.* Norman, OK: University of Oklahoma Press, 1967.

Wharfield, H. B. *Fort Yuma on the Colorado River.* El Cajon, CA: H. B. Wharfield, 1968.

DISCOVER THOUSANDS OF LOCAL HISTORY BOOKS FEATURING MILLIONS OF VINTAGE IMAGES

Arcadia Publishing, the leading local history publisher in the United States, is committed to making history accessible and meaningful through publishing books that celebrate and preserve the heritage of America's people and places.

Find more books like this at
www.arcadiapublishing.com

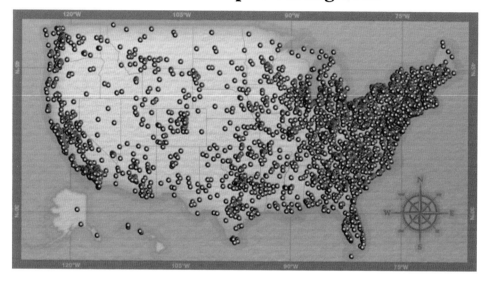

Search for your hometown history, your old stomping grounds, and even your favorite sports team.

Consistent with our mission to preserve history on a local level, this book was printed in South Carolina on American-made paper and manufactured entirely in the United States. Products carrying the accredited Forest Stewardship Council (FSC) label are printed on 100 percent FSC-certified paper.

MADE IN THE